CORRESPONDENCE IN ASTROLOGY,

A PATH TO OUR TRUE SELF

IRENE RIMER

October 28, 2016

Acknowledgement

I wish to express my gratitude to God for taking me from where I was, to put me back where I belong, in His presence.

Table of Contents

Introduction

There was once a six-year-old girl who asked her Mom, who are we, where do we come from, and where are we going. "I don't know. In fact, no one really knows," Mom said. This was very confusing to the little girl as she deeply felt there was so much more. That little girl full of questions was this writer.

It was on my seventh birthday when my curiosity in the occult started after having an "out of body" experience. Dad, a well-respected attorney and political figure in our town, had organized a party to celebrate my birthday. Father hired musicians, cooks, and over 100 guests were expected. I was counting the days to my birthday, and was extremely excited thinking about the shower of gifts that were coming my way. However, when the day came, the party had to be cancelled. Earlier that morning, I started complaining of pain in the intestinal area. As the day progressed, the pain increased to the point I began to scream. Mom noticed my belly was swollen and felt a sense of urgency; she called Dr.

Santaella, a friend of the family, who came over our home and after checking me rushed me to the hospital. Upon arriving at the emergency room, the usual doctor on call was not available; instead Dr. Ardila, was in charge that day. This doctor, nicknamed "the butcher," had a reputation of being very bold because he would not wait for analysis of blood tests to operate on a patient when he "felt" they were in real danger. On top of this, at the time, the father's authority to operate on a child was required where we lived. The mother's signature was not enough; and father, who didn't know what was happening, could not be reached by phone. Doctor Santaella feared the operation couldn't wait, and assuming all responsibility, authorized Dr. Ardila, who didn't hesitate, to intervene immediately. This would have probably never happened today, much less in the US.

I remember being carried on a bed to the operating room where the doctor placed an ugly black mask on my face. I fought everyone restraining me until I just couldn't. I don't recall what happened right after going under anesthesia; but all of a sudden I clearly remember to this day sitting on the operating table, turning my head to the right, and looking at the doctor. He had a dark green operating mask on his face, and was removing a piece of intestine with a surgical tweezer; he handed it over to a helper who placed it inside a jar filled with a solution that looked like water to me. Immediately after that, I moved forward going through the wall in front of me; a long entrance hall to the hospital was on the other side of the operating room. The day was bright; it must have been sometime between noon and 3 PM. I kept going forward, and noticed I was not walking, but displacing myself in the air. However, this was no surprise to me. On the contrary, it felt normal and as if I had done it before. Close to the end of the hall, by the main entrance to the hospital, there was an old lady talking to a young man; I instinctively knew it was a grandmother talking to her grandchild. Next, when I opened my eyes, I was in a room and noticed my hands were tied to the rails of the bed, so I would not pull the three tubes going into my body from my nostrils and mouth. When I told the doctor what I had seen during the operation, he told me I must have been dreaming since I was totally asleep. I later found out I was clinically dead for a few minutes.

If this was a dream, it was unlike any other I had before; deep down in my heart I knew this experience had given me a clue of another world, I couldn't explain, a spiritual existence. I knew that regardless of the life of my body, I had another body that could fly.

When my family moved to the US, my curiosity became dormant as daily life activities and goals took center stage in my life. At times, however, I felt as if I were falling into a vacuum, empty. When I received word that my paternal grandfather had passed, and that in his will he had requested that one of his children go to Israel to inform his family of his passing, I volunteered to go. At that time, I was enrolled in a Business Master's program at Barry University in Miami that offered credits for attending classes at the Hebrew University in Jerusalem. So, I took the opportunity to get the credits; and at the same time, visit the family fulfilling grandfather's wishes. At the time, mother had become a Christian; and whenever she would attempt to talk to me about her new faith, I would reject her. Before going on my trip to Israel, I felt bad about the way I had treated her; I asked Mom to give me a bible for my birthday, and promised to read it to prove to her that it was nonsense.

From the time the school trimester had ended, to the time I was scheduled to go to Jerusalem, I had plenty of time to read. Mother ordered the bible, dedicated it, and gave it to me. Even though I wanted to prove something, I started to read with a good attitude; because at least I was not afraid, if proven wrong, to change my mind.

The reading sometimes was extremely boring and I thought of quitting; more so during parts of the book about generations, of generations. It seemed an unending account of people through time for no reason. A force, I didn't understand, however, pushed me to keep on reading, not allowing me to stop; to the point I started to connect the days and nights. Some things I thought I understood, some things I didn't, but kept on reading. I reread some parts; went forward, went back, and finished.

I had not formed an opinion on anything I had read as I arrived at Mount Scopus in Jerusalem, where the dorms of the Hebrew University are located. The following weekend, I went on a tour to the Wailing Wall. It was around 3 PM, and the sun's light was hitting the rocks of the old city making them look as if made of gold. The thought of this city being called "Jerusalem of Gold" came to mind. I felt uplifted and smelled white flowers that only grow in that part of the world. Then as I looked at the wall, I beheld the entrance to Solomon's temple right in front of my eyes. There was a tall man walking peacefully by the majestic colonnades. Then a voice in my mind came as an inaudible impression that said, "Schlomit, (my name in Hebrew meaning peace,) I am Jeshua."

Seven days after returning from my trip to Israel, I had a dream I couldn't understand at first. I had woken up with the taste of salt on my lips. Throughout the following week, I searched in the bible for clues into the meaning of the dream; and as I opened it randomly, the pages where the answers were turned one by one. I realized the bible really had an internal sense; and that the dream was a confirmation. I was now part of the salt of the earth as indicated in the book where it says: "ye are the salt of the earth" *(Matthew 5:13)*. The door to the spiritual kingdom had opened, and this was a new beginning for me. Needless to say, the only thing I proved was that I was wrong; and, that somehow, this "force", that is God, kept on giving me experiences, dreams, and visions, and wouldn't let me stop reading. He was communicating with me through the divine Law of Correspondence which I will expose in this thesis as the way in which nature communicates with us.

The reason I mention some of my experiences is to make an important point. As we go through life, we are given dreams and experiences as tokens to treasure. These are really messages from within that reveal our uniqueness, and also our oneness. They reveal individual purpose in life. I kept all my tokens in my heart.

As time passed, life got me distracted in other matters, such as working, getting married, having children, and then a divorce. It was in 2011, with a wrinkled heart, that the force in me lead me into discovering Astrology.

Alice Bailey calls Astrology "the greatest and oldest of all sciences" *(3)*. Astrologer Marc Edmond Jones often said, "Astrology is the science of all beginnings." I have come to realize that the logic of the stars spells out secrets of the soul to the one that learns the language of the universe; it also offers a way to help ourselves and others. To the one willing to accept and perceive its transformative gifts, it offers a path into mysticism; into rising above the wheel of matter, self-knowledge, and the discovery of our Inner self, our real identity.

In this thesis, I will expound on the greatness of astrology as it is all about the Law of Correspondence. It is an intellectual path where concentration and analysis are required; therefore, the training of the mind is essential.

Three basic approaches to astrology will be stated; but I will

only focus on the one dealing with the archetypes of the

zodiac by briefly describing some of the relationships

established within astrology by correspondence using the

planets, signs, and their interaction. In this thesis it will be

shown how this divine language uncovers the twelve basic

personalities of the Personal self within the unconscious

mind; and how by analysis and synthesis, the True self may

be revealed, when we are willing to enter the spiritual path.

Review of Literature

According to Dr. Paul Leon Masters, one can receive no greater gift than the gift of metaphysical knowledge. As Socrates notably said, "The unexplained life is not worth living" *(Master's Curriculum 2:03).*

For a human being coming to this world, seeking the answers to the questions of who they are, what they are, and where they are going, can mean many years of living with a feeling of being lost or falling into a vacuum, as I did. The person may get so deep into the affairs of the world, and the Personal self, that they may never perceive internally that there is more; or, if he or she does slightly perceive it, they may never find answers in this lifetime; unless the person is open to receive the inner guidance within us at all times.

We come to this world naked, imbued in a body of matter, under the "veils of illusion." As when we partially submerge a perfectly straight stick under water, the deeper we submerge it, the more we see it bent or broken from outside because we do not perceive truth with the physical eye, but illusions. Therefore, we cannot see what our physical eyes are not able to perceive. In order to "see" beyond this dense world, we must develop spiritual sight.

Jesus Christ said that the kingdom of heaven is within each of us. He further told us what to do to gain access to it. "When thou prayest, enter into thy closet, shut the door behind thee, and prayeth to the Father, which seeth in secret. These words not easily perceived to the regular sense of hearing…are understandable to any mystic" *(Master's Curriculum 2:11).*

Most people in the world believe we can never have the answers of what we cannot perceive with our physical senses; however, mystics throughout the centuries have delved into the basic questions of life, and through inner searching have found answers. They have gone into the quietness of their deep minds, and have discovered the inner world in which all answers are found; answers not only satisfactory to the heart, but to the intellect as well.

But, what is required to be a mystic?

After years of self-searching, personal study and experiences, I can say today that the key to mysticism is meditation; and a willingness to be open to receive internal guidance through life is required because the search for truth has to start within ourselves. No one else can do it for us. If initially we do not understand that the simplest way to gain wisdom is through practical mysticism, there are other ways that can lead us to spirituality. We can become mystics ourselves in the process of learning what they have learned through the following of an intellectual path. Astrology, which means star logic, offers one of these intellectual paths. Its essence is based on the universal Law of Correspondence.

The divine Law of Correspondence is clearly expressed in the occult maxim widely known and used by mystic astrologers, and attributed to Hermes Trismegistus, that states "as above, so below, as within, so without, as the universe, so the soul." The meaning of this is that all that is on earth is but a reflection of what is above. Also, that all that is outside of one's self is a reflection of what is within; that the causes are above or within, and the effects are below or without; and, because of this, there is harmony "between the physical, mental and spiritual realms. There is no separation since everything in the Universe, including you, originates from the One Source. The same pattern is expressed on all planes of existence from the smallest electron to the largest star and vice versa. All is One" *(Kotsos).*

"Metaphysical religious teachings are based upon insight gained by mystics, down through the ages, in higher states of spiritual consciousness in meditation" *(Master's Curriculum 2:55).* The bible, for example, has been widely misinterpreted because of lack of spiritual insight of those who read it, and want to explain it literally. It is stated in many parts of the good book that eyes are required to see, and ears to hear. He who cannot see and hear through the spiritual senses does not understand or perceive what's written in the scriptures because the bible is written with an internal meaning that requires internal senses of perception. Its language is spiritual.

In the book *Heaven and its Wonders and Hell,*

translated from the original Latin by John C. Ager, and

written by one of the greatest mystics of all ages, Emanuel

Swedenborg wrote that those who believe all the words of the

bible literally,

"…are ignorant of the arcana that lie hid in every
particular of the Word. For in every particular of the
Word there is an internal sense which treats of
things spiritual and heavenly, not of things natural
and worldly… And this is true not only of the
meaning of groups of words, it is true of each
particular word. For the Word is written solely by
correspondences, to the end that there may be an
internal sense in every least particular of it" *(88)*.

A dual meaning in a word according to the

perception of the senses would be the meaning of the word

"light." Light, for example, in the spiritual sense means inner

understanding. All we can see on earth has an internal

understanding that corresponds to the spiritual kingdom.

According to Swedenborg, God is the invisible sun

that gives spiritual illumination to man; and this spiritual

light, reflected by all other bodies of the celestial realm as

well, is the light of his understanding. The eye that can

perceive this truth is the internal sight. Therefore, by correspondence, understanding has light from heaven, the same way that external sight has light from the sun of the world. In the conjunction of the material and spiritual worlds within man, the light of heaven that originates with God, is always within men; but it flows into man only in the degree that he is receptive; and vibrates towards truth, or is united with it. This means that to perceive the light of heaven is to be enlightened; because in the same manner that the sight of the eye has extension into the material world, internal sight, which is the light of the understanding, has extension into the spiritual world.

Jesus said that the kingdom of heaven is within each of us. This, again, means that within man there is a conjunction, or an overlapping, of the material and the spiritual kingdoms; that we not only have a physical body, but a spiritual body as well; and that the physical body is perishable, but the spiritual body is not. This is profound when we realize that, through life and each day, we carry heaven, as well as hell, within ourselves; that everything invisible to the bare eye can also be perceived by man; but the perception must be internal to realize that out of the invisible comes all that is visible. All that is unseen is manifested in nature by correspondence.

A "sensual" person is one that can only see with physical eyes. He "may appear to be divinely inspired, the fanatic, in his emotional zeal, nonetheless misquotes the words of God because he lacks the authentic inner understanding of the Bible that is only possessed by the true Mystic" *(Master's Curriculum 2:57)*. This person is closed to the spiritual world and fails to perceive internally that the bible is written by correspondence. The Law of Correspondence is in all we see, including the letters of our alphabets, the numbers, geometry, and mathematics.

Kabbalist Daniel C. Matt explains correspondence like this:

"If God spoke the world into being, the divine language is energy: the alphabet, elementary particles; God's grammar, the laws of nature" *(Loc. 1296).*

Correspondence is the language of Heaven. Let us be guided by the understanding of this language of nature, which relates spiritual things to man in ways he can understand; so that we can see the things that exist in the external world, and through these things, know the spiritual world; because unless a man is raised above the senses of perception of the material world, the external man does not have internal sight or the wisdom to make the connection from the spiritual, invisible, to the worldly, material.

The great Pythagoras used correspondence when he invented the musical scale, although he was no musician. This writer accounts for the fascinating story of how Pythagoras made the connection of the frequency of sound, weight, mathematics, and finally the planets of the cosmos to come up with his *"Music of the Spheres"* and the diatonic musical scale of seven notes in her book titled *Universal Flamenco*.

Claudius Ptolemy, who is considered to be the father of modern astrology, also used correspondence. "He was influenced by the numerology of the Greek philosopher Pythagoras who sought mathematical harmonies in the universe and developed a mathematical theory of music" *(Louis 8)*.

Ptolemy combined Pythagoras' theory with his knowledge of astronomy and ancient astrology to come up with a theory of astrological relationships based on form and numbers. He called these relationships "aspects." These aspects are geometrical patterns, at specific distances, the planets make with one another as they travel on their orbits through space, in relationship to the signs of the zodiac, and over different areas of the circumference of the earth. These aspects that form in heaven reveal the modes of operation of energy forces that influence everything on earth, including our minds on the subconscious plane. Ptolemy recognized four aspects to be "major" aspects because these repeat the same harmonic ratios of Pythagoras musical scale.

As described by Stephanie Jean Clements, "an aspect is a combination of two planets, and the interaction of the two planets occurs because of a specific angular distance between them" *(American Federation of Astrologers Lesson 8)*. Thousands and thousands of years of studies, and spiritual insights, accounted for in records from generations of astrologers to subsequent generations, indicate, for example, that the square aspect is challenging, or difficult. This means that when in a natal horoscope, two planets are 90 degrees from each other within the zodiac, which follows the curvature of the earth, forming the angle of a square, certain obstacles must be overcome in life. If you meditate on a square, you may realize that the straight lines have to radically bend within this shape to change course in L shapes. If you imagine energy travelling through these lines, the changes at angles do not represent an easy "flow" but a forced change of direction, obstacles. Let me point out to the reader, however, that he who has internal sight can sense, and feel, the square aspect as "difficult" energies without having to do astrological calculations.

To the one who has not developed internal sight, astrology uncovers a book of nature we can see with our bare eyes in the starry heaven because it is written as though with bright red ink upon a piece of paper on the sky. To the intellectual, discovering the mechanics of the language of the stars can be perplexing as there is a lot of geometry and mathematics involved, making this process very objective, and even scientific. As we learn in astrology, even a skeptic at first cannot for long help but notice the universe may be trying to convey meaning through a mechanical method because of the use of numbers, and flawless mathematics. When instead of revolving around the mechanics, we allow the internal significance of astrology to come forth, we get enlightened, as the deeper meaning will activate deeper lessons that will offer guidance into developing our internal senses. What the Mystic learns is a divine correspondence within geometry and mathematics; and, this is more enlightening. We can then learn through an intellectual mechanical process what we also feel intuitively, to the point where we will just know. The secrets will be revealed one by one because the stars love to gossip!

Although we are truly justified when we refer to astrology as a science, we stand quite away from what is generally considered a science, implying technology based on the scientific method, because there is already equipment that can go beyond what the physical eye can see; but it cannot go far beyond this physical kingdom. As of today, there is no scientific equipment that can detect anything in the world of spirits that would give us a clue on how this world influences the human mind. Machines cannot penetrate the spiritual world; because in order to be able to enter another world, we must have a body that can function in that world. There is a center in continuous degrees, that seem to have no ending, that divides the material from the immaterial. This idea can be intellectually illustrated by the correspondence with numbers, and using the Law of Polarity. When counting down from positive numbers to zero, in order to continue from the positive tangible to the intangible side, we must change the mathematical sign to negative; this is easily illustrated by just looking at the numbers: 3, 2, 1, 0, -1, -2, -3. Something tangible that can also give us a perspective of the Law of Correspondence is a mirror; where all that is seen from one side is seen in the opposite side, but in reversed position. Remember what Hermes said, "...from within, without."

"Astrology is the science that explores the correlations between celestial bodies and animate and inanimate objects. Astrology has its place among the earliest records of human learning. It is the parent of astronomy; for many years they were one science...the charting of the horoscope is really an astronomical process; the judgement or delineation of the horoscope is an astrological process" (March 1).

In astrology, we deal with unseen energy, magnetism, influencing people's psyche. Most astrologers are not mystics, however, most fail to go deeper into the insight astrology offers about the spiritual world; and how a person can transcend his or her current state and circumstances in the world of matter, to gain self-mastery through understanding more about it. This writer has been in many conferences and workshops with world-recognized astrologers that seem to be able to answer all questions, except the most important ones; those related to the essence of the human soul. Some seem to be going in circles, but are not able to rise above it, in spite of all the intellectual knowledge they possess.

Alice Bailey states in *Esoteric Astrology*: "astrology has not really proved itself to the world of thought and science, in spite of many definitely demonstrable successes." *(Bailey, 1:01)*. Astrology is a science that has been demonized, ridiculed, and misunderstood mainly by controlling powers that do not want people to be empowered by knowledge, because unfortunately the more ignorant people are, the easier it is to control them. In addition, unfortunately, there are a large number of astrologers that are not spiritual; and some are only inspired by money. These astrologers are not able to perceive the essence, the spiritual meaning, of what is right in front of their eyes; a divine guide through the wheel of physical existence. Therefore, being an astrologer does not make anyone a mystic; there is only knowledge without the wisdom to use it wisely.

Bailey, who spoke of astrology as being the greatest and oldest of all sciences, and essential as "the purest presentation of occult truth in the world," made the case that "Astrology is a science which must be restored to its original beauty and truth before the world can gain a truer perspective and appreciation of the divine plan, as it is expressed at this time through the Wisdom of the Ages" *(1:01)*.

In the book titled *Simplified Scientific Astrology*, Max Heindel beautifully wrote about the correspondence of the stars with the life of men, and the power we can have with

this knowledge:

"There is an invisible part of man which exerts a powerful
influence in life, and as the tides are measured by the motion
of the Sun and Moon, so also the eventualities of existence
are measured by the circling stars, which may therefore be
called the "clock of Destiny," and knowledge of their import
is an immense power, for to the competent astrologer the
horoscope reveals every secret of life" *(5)*.

Astrology is profound as it truly reveals the

relationship of the universe to all things on earth.

Unfortunately, its powers of personal transformation are

often overlooked by most of the astrologers who are able to

understand this science intellectually, but not spiritually.

The reason I say that most astrologers understand this

science intellectually, although they are not spiritual, is

because astrology is really a mental path that requires a lot of

training in order to be able to do calculations and deep

analysis. The mathematics involved is not as complicated as

some think; however, the concepts do require study and

practice. Concentration is needed for the understanding of the

association of ideas, coupled with good research skills.

Therefore, a collected mind is essential for designing the plan sheets that are regularly prepared for the interpretation of astrological charts. As the astrologer gains practice in the use of numbers, geometry, and associations in doing analysis, flashes of intuition are perceived; and its development is experienced exponentially.

Generally, astrologers focus on the work needed; and most emphasize on the mechanics to prepare accurate horoscopes, and analyze the energies that interplay within these horoscopes. However, by missing the point, they fail to seek the source from where these energies originate. This is similar to what a student of meditation goes through when instead of focusing on the relationship to the Inner self, the source of everything good, they focus on the images of the astral world, or on finding out about past lives, future lives, or telepathy. They go out of focus missing the most important goal which is union with God; because all goes forth from the center that contains it all within.

Truth will come forth, however, to more and more people sooner than we think with the advances in science because, at the end of the day, science will only prove true what the Mystics of the ages already know. "Ultimately, the Metaphysical and the Empirical will be in harmony as humankind evolves, and outer science discovers that the farthest reaches of Infinity, or outer space, equal the Inner Infinite Depths of the human mind" *(Master's Curriculum 2:36)*. The essence of astrology will be restored and recognized as the true science. "Esoteric Astrology" as this essence is known offers proof that this ancient discipline reveals truth as it is about "…the Life and Lives which inform the "points of light" within the universal Life" *(Bailey 1:08)*. It deals with the manifestation of energy in all states within the cosmos.

There are different approaches to astrology. One is the conscious-intellectual approach which is often considered to be empirical because it is based on psychological observations; however, these observations often make astrology be portrayed as superficial. The Cosmo-biological approach attempts to make it objective by connecting the motion of the planets to the rhythms of the human body, and to the human organs. Many doctors will start to discover how astrology can be part of diagnosis and treating diseases. This is indeed effective in the practice of medicine and its applications as revealed by many studies conducted in the 1900s by Dr. Reinhold Ebertin, who according to the online *Wikipedia* encyclopedia, and many other sources, is considered to have founded modern Cosmo-biology. This approach, however, does not reveal the path astrology offers into the deepest hidden motivation of the human soul which is that of finding the True self through the channel that connects us to the inner world.

The ancient approach of using the gods of the Mythology of many ancient civilizations, the zodiac signs, and the planets, in astrology, to explain the different personalities within the unconscious mind, offers a deep understanding of ourselves. This approach reveals that the personalities of these gods described in ancient stories really contain historical references that account for the development of thought and the psyche of human beings.

"In order to make simple the great truths of Nature and the abstract principles of natural law, the vital forces of the universe were personified, becoming the gods and goddesses of the ancient mythologies." *(Hall. Loc. 865)*

Myths are like parables. They help people to understand concepts. They explain the meaning or purpose of life without which there is a feeling of emptiness. Myths are not only good for describing characters, they also guide mental processes, and influence the way we think, and also how we perceive. "Myths come to life by serving as models for human behavior." *(Matt. Loc. 1352-1353)*.

As noted by Dr. Paul Leon Masters, Swiss psychiatrist, Carl Jung, "…explored the teachings of the mystics and metaphysicians who existed throughout the ages, in an attempt to penetrate the deepest layers of the human mind" *(Master's Curriculum 2:03)*; and, incorporated into the field of psychology the teachings of these mystics with the concept of what he called The Archetypes. The term "archetype" originates from the combination of two Greek root words, *archein*, which means "original or old"; and *typos*, or "type."

There is no doubt in this writer's mind that by applying the Law of Correspondence, Jung associated the gods of mythology, also within astrology, with the personalities of men. He recognized them as forces within the unconscious mind. The mystics have been teaching about these "forces" for ages by the use of mythology, and the zodiac, in stories and books containing internal meaning. They have done this to reveal truth to whoever could assimilate it, and disguise it from those that could not.

As there are 12 tribes of Israel, 12 labors of Jupiter, 12 disciples of Jesus, and 12 basic archetypes as defined by Jung, there are 12 signs of the zodiac from which all these 12 originate. Out of the combination of these original archetypes, many others are revealed. By grouping them, we can also uncover similarities in the motivations of these archetypes, or personalities.

Psychotherapist, Carl Golden, makes a significant connection between the *12 Common Archetypes* in mythology and the emotions within men: "Archetypes represent fundamental human motifs of our experience as we evolve; consequentially, they evoke deep emotions".

Planets reflect back to earth, and among themselves, the light vibrations of the Sun in different frequencies we distinguish as colors and shades in the physical realm. As there are seven seen colors of the rainbow, seven notes in the diatonic musical scale, seven Universal Laws, there are seven planets that are closer to earth. These have been called the "Seven Spirits before the throne," and each planet is said to excerpt a special influence over the seven endocrine glands in the human body; and all areas of human activity. As man's consciousness evolves, he opens up to the influence of the outer planets. The planets, which reflect the light of the sun and are personified within the gods in myth, are modified by the 12 signs of the zodiac according to their position, as they travel through space displacing the ether, and sending out their vibrations.

As noted in the first volume of my favorite set of books for the beginner astrologer or amateur, *The Only Way to Learn Astrology*, "each sign is a field of action in which the planetary forces operate. Each sign has a full range of possibilities, and the individual has the option of using what the sign indicates in a positive or beneficial manner, on one hand, or in a negative or abusive fashion on the other" *(March 12)*. Therefore, in astrology, we are often told to view the planets as "actors" and the signs as "characters" the actors portray.

The zodiac signs, characters, can be grouped by elements, and also by modality, indicating the manner in which they work. For example, if we take the 12 signs, and divide them by four, ancient knowledge has revealed these groupings of 3 times 4 correspond to the four elements, fire, earth, air, and water; which are expressions of matter originating from one primal source, as the light of the Sun is one. Therefore, 3 signs fall under the element of fire, 3 signs fall under the element of earth, and so forth. When dividing the 12 signs by three, the modality or manner in which these elements work will be uncovered. 4 x 3 are four signs grouped under the modes of cardinal, fixed, or flexible. This means that 4 signs are cardinal, 4 are fixed, and 4 are flexible or adaptable. A final division by 2, uncovers the polarity of the signs. They can be either active, positive, and masculine; or passive, negative, and feminine. 6 signs are positive, and 6 are negative. Starting from the first sign, Aries is, fire, cardinal, and positive. Taurus is feminine, earth, and fixed. Gemini is air, flexible, and masculine. Cancer is water, cardinal, and feminine, and so forth.

To explain how the above information can be used, "…Aries is bold and dynamic. The Moon represents the emotions, and when the Moon is in Aries we would expect that person to express emotions in a bold and dynamic manner. If Mercury is in Aries, we would expect the individual to reason and think boldly and dynamically, because Mercury has to do with thinking and reasoning" *(March 11).* .

To further illustrate, if a planet falls within a sign in the element of water, and into the fixed mode, the astrologer will conclude that the planet is in the sign of Scorpio; and will behave as an archetype associated to that planet and sign. The element of water indicates an emotional sign; the fixed mode indicates lack of activity and inflexibility. If we then were to imagine "fixed water" we would not think of a river, which would describe the cardinal mode in water, but a stagnant pond; fixed and unmovable.

Scorpio people may have the positive characteristics of being motivated, penetrating, private, scientific, investigative, probing, and passionate; and/or the negative characteristics of tending to be vengeful, secretive, violent, sarcastic, suspicious, jealous, and intolerant. Therefore, according to *metaphysicalzone.com,* the archetypes of "The Detective, The Sorcerer, and/or The Hypnotist" may be attributed to this sign. I want to remind the reader that the characteristics of the sign may be accentuated for good or for bad according to aspects to other planets determined by the position of the planets at the moment of birth.

As mentioned, the archetypes that fall under the groups of signs according to elements, modalities, and polarity, reveal common driving sources. Aspects determine the nature of the circumstances to be encountered. "Thousands of years of research have established that certain mental factors in the subconscious mind of man become active when certain planets are aspected in the sky" *(Astrology's Wide Influence, X)*. These revelations are mystical truths within astrology. By knowing about astrological associations, we can find deep secrets about anyone, anything, or ourselves.

To briefly describe how this analysis is used in astrology, Aries, the first sign of the horoscope, for example, is said to be ruled by the planet Mars, which is seen as "acting" as the Greek God Ares, or the Roman God Mars, in mythology. Wherever Mars is within a horoscope, that's where the person puts his or her greatest energy because Ares, Mars, is the god of war. If aspects to Mars are harmonious in an astrological chart, the person, may behave with the positive characteristics of the sign of Aries; active, energetic, and courageous. The energy will be harmonious. If on the contrary, aspects are challenging, the person may lack courage, have a "me first" attitude, be selfish, or even a coward; he will behave according to the negative traits that correspond to that sign. To show how much astrology covers, let me add here that in anatomy, Aries is, by correspondence, associated with the head and the face. This is surely related to what the bible says in Corinthians 1:12:

"For the body is not one member, but many. If the foot says, "Because I am not a hand, I am not a part of the body," it is not for this reason any the less a part of the body. And if the ear says, "Because I am not an eye, I am not a part of the body," it is not for this reason any the less a part of the body. If the whole body were an eye, where would the hearing be? If the whole were hearing, where would the sense of smell be? But now God has placed the members, each one of them, in the body, just as He desired. If they were all one member, where would the body be? But now there are many members, but one body" *(NIV)*.

The zodiac signs of Taurus and Libra are both ruled by Venus, "the Goddess of Love." Venus will then behave for good, or for bad, according to the traits of the two signs. Taurus, the second sign, corresponds to the throat and neck; Libra, the seventh sign, corresponds to the kidneys. Gemini and Virgo are ruled by the planet Mercury, the architype Hermes, associated with the intellect, communication abilities, teaching and learning as well as with messengers, electronics, computers, and merchants in business. In the body, the third sign of Gemini corresponds to the lungs, hands, and arms; and, the sixth sign of Virgo corresponds to the intestinal area. The eighth sign, Scorpio, is ruled by Mars, and also Pluto that correspond respectively to the gods Ares and Hades in myth. In anatomy, Scorpio corresponds to the genital area, and the organs of excretion. Sagittarius is the ninth sign, and Pisces is the twelfth sign. They are ruled by the planet Jupiter, related to Hercules, also Zeus, in mythology. Neptune, one of the outer planets, is also a co-ruler of Pisces, and is associated with Poseidon, the sea god. It is said that few people on earth are able to perceive vibrations from this planet as it is related to the spiritual world, to mysticism. In anatomy, Sagittarius corresponds to the hips and thighs, and Pisces to the feet. The eleventh sign that corresponds to the ankles is Aquarius ruled by Saturn, the God of time; it is also co-ruled by Uranus, another outer planet, representing "The Awakener," "The Rebel", or "The Humanitarian." Cancer, the fourth sign corresponds to the breast and the stomach; and is associated with "The Mother" archetype ruled by the Moon representing the emotions, as well as domestic, and nurturing urges; the Moon has been personified by "Selene" in Greek, and "Luna" in Roman, mythology. The fifth sign of Leo that corresponds to the heart, associated with the archetypes of "the God Apollo" and "The Authority," is ruled by the Sun. Let me add that this sign also represents the urge to shine, the personality, or ego. Leo indicates the qualities of leadership in a person. The tenth sign is Capricorn that corresponds to the knees and the skeleton. The planet Saturn, Chronos, the keeper of time, rules this sign. It represents our urge for security and safety. It also represents karma, and death. The signs of the zodiac and the planets also correspond to colors, minerals, plants, animals, places on earth, to name a few things.

Remember, each planet represents an archetype behaving according to the sign where they are placed, for good or for bad depending on the aspects or relationship between and among the other planets. The natal chart with the aspects are calculated at the time of birth, because it is at this time, more specifically from the moment the baby inhales his or her first breath, when the vibrations within the atmosphere of that specific moment and place are first absorbed by the babies' lungs, as the soul is manifested on the physical universe at its appointed time. Additional calculations may subsequently be done to know more about the progressions of the planets which indicate the appointed time we are to pay our debts or receive our rewards in this life-time according to The Law of Karma. This, however, is another topic for discussion.

The 12 inner basic personalities that influence our subconscious mind, as pointed out in *The Personality Charts*, "can relate to each other, and these relations turn into independent personalities themselves…" And, if each relationship creates a variance in personality, a new archetype is created; so, we can have many more individual personalities. If we want to know more about a life, the influencing archetypes within a particular person's subconscious mind, or ourselves for that matter, we examine the position of the planets, by zodiac sign, and aspects. Other considerations are to be taken such as the minor influences of other bodies in space; however, this writer cannot cover all astrology can give. As the reader can see, it really encompasses it all. Whatever we want to find out is there.

In an unpublished article that my friend, astrologer Bob Mulligan, shared with me, he wrote that the planetary energies of astrology are actually deities who have a special function in creation. That one way of advancing spiritually is to become friends with the planetary gods and goddesses. When our mind (associated to the planet Mercury in astrology) is still, "we could hear what these gods and goddesses say." After all, Mercury, related to Hermes, the archetype, is "the messenger of the gods" in mythology. He further wrote that "dialoguing with the planets is like journaling inasmuch as they help us access deeper aspects of reality. When we develop friendships within a higher kingdom of creation exponentially expanding our understanding, or what we do with our clients, transforms us."

"Astrology has a key, which when used before entering human relationships ...tells of the attraction or repulsion of the personalities. This whole subject is tied in with the horoscope in many of its facets—aspects from one chart to the other, affinity or interests through house comparison, similar motivation through zodiacal sign comparison, and so on" *(The Versatility of Astrology 29)*.

By understanding the seen and unseen talents and short-comings in the different charts of people, we can gain insight for spiritual growth, and "...becoming aware of the multifaceted unity can help us learn how to live in harmony with other human beings and with all beings" *(Matt. Loc. 1369)*. This sums up the practical use of astrology.

Discussion

In astrology, as we have already covered previously, we can determine the characteristics of a person's hidden forces, the archetypes, by locating the position of the planets in a person's horoscope. The first architype, "The Warrior" is an archetype that clearly is related to the attributes of the first sign of the zodiac, Aries. If we want to know about a person's strength, the ability to assert himself or herself in the outer world, their fighting style, and if they have courage or lack it, all we have to do is to locate the position of the planet Mars, the god of war, in their horoscope. Depending on the sign and aspects to other planets, we will have an idea of where and how the "warrior" is within a person's subconscious mind. If Mars is located in the sign of Sagittarius, the person may be overly religious; religiosity being associated with the sign of Sagittarius. These associations of archetypes to planets, and signs, with the aspects involved, may be difficult to do; but after a while, one can easily make the connections as they start to be felt by intuition once there is familiarity with the characteristics and concepts involved.

The second subconscious personality related to the sign of Taurus is "The Beautiful." If we want to find out about security or insecurities, values and self-worth, sensuality, capacity to enjoy possessions and friendships, and even sexual desire, we should find the location of Venus in the chart. "The Intellectual" is the third personality and is related to the sign of Gemini and the planet Mercury. It indicates our intellectual capacity. "The Mother," or "The Family," related to the sign of Cancer is personality number four; and it is indicated by the Moon's position. "The Hero" is the fifth personality, associated with the sign of Leo, and it describes the vitality, ego, and life force. "Reason" is the sixth personality, related to the sign of Virgo. This personality indicates how a person adapts, and deals with his or her needs; it also gives us insights into what we have to accept in life. This archetype is found by locating the planet Mercury in the chart, and by looking at the aspects. The seventh personality, related to the sign of Libra, is "The Balance," or "The Other." This one tells us about our relationships with other people, our parents, our spouse or meaningful other, and the world. Venus' position will give us this insight into these areas. Related to the sign of Scorpio is "The Sorcerer." The eighth personality indicates how we deal with the gods of the underworld, our hidden desires, and the forces of death. This influence can be found looking for the planet Mars; and also Pluto. The ninth personality, associated with the sign of Sagittarius, is "The Philosopher" which describes the counselor within, and the role of religion within the life being examined. To know about this archetype, we look at the position of the planet Jupiter, "Thor" in Norse Myth or "Zeus." The tenth personality is "The Teacher" or "The Old Man or Woman." This archetype is related to the planet Saturn and the sign of Capricorn. It describes our career, our vocation, and if we are disciplined or not. As already mentioned, Saturn is the planet of death, karma, and the truth fate wants to teach us. Also, associated with the planet Saturn, and with Uranus, and the sign of Aquarius, is "The Liberator," the eleventh archetype. It describes our views on humanity, liberty, and independence. The twelfth, and last basic personality in astrology is "The Master" associated with the planets Jupiter and Neptune, as well as the sign of Pisces. This archetype tells us about the world of illusion, things that are hidden from our sight, and about our spiritual life.

As the reader can see from the brief explanation given on the relationships between the archetypes, the planets, and the zodiac signs, astrology can provide a vast amount of information. It reveals patterns from our past that we have a tendency to repeat; it also shows us that our past shapes our future. Therefore, if we know the real cause of an event, we can be prepared, and forearmed, to make adjustments by negating and cancelling those patterns, when they are negative. Not only do we have an opportunity of learning about individual souls and ourselves, but on the circumstances, and the fate, that affect entire countries, because countries and events have origins; therefore, charts can be created for them. Through astrology, small and big answers are provided. From finding out where we dropped our precious gold ring, and if we can recover it; to details of our past, the falling of empires, and the rising of new ones.

One of the astrological charts this writer has enjoyed the most studying has been the birth chart of Galileo Galilei, the Italian scientist born in the 17th century. He unlocked secrets of astronomy and the natural motion of objects. Galileo designed and built the first high-powered astronomical telescope; demonstrated the speed of falling objects are not proportional to their weights; came up with many of the ideas behind Newton's laws of motion; and demonstrated what we know as the Copernican theory of the solar system. Galileo tried to demonstrate that the planets revolve around the sun, and not the Earth, as it was believed at the time he lived. Nevertheless, He had to deal with an insolent society who did not care to see the truth in spite of overwhelming evidence he was ready to show with his new telescope. The Roman church accused Galileo of being a heretic. He was forced to renounce the truth publicly or die. Eventually, research proved Galileo's theories to be correct. "The Vatican officially recognized the validity of Galileo's work in 1993… Others had invented very low-power telescopes before Galileo, but he refined and improved the idea so greatly that he is generally considered the inventor of the modern telescope" *(Who2)*.

The official life of Galileo falls short of all the information this writer gathered from analyzing this man's life through the use of astrology. Galileo followed his heart against a great deal of challenges, and opposition--some of the aspects within astrology. His father wanted him to go to Medical School; and although Galileo enrolled in school with the intention of making his father proud, he soon changed professions when he started to notice things in nature that intrigued him. He fathered one son, and two daughters from a relationship with a woman he loved even though he couldn't marry because she was not of his same social status. Because his children were the product of an "out of marriage relationship," only his son was able to marry into society; however, he had to send his daughters to a monastery because no one would marry them. His horoscope reveals his daughters respected, admired, and loved him very much because they understood he did the best he could do for them. Galileo's chart reveals his emotions, his drive, and his path. In dealing with the people of the time, he was deeply frustrated. During the last years of his life, while in house prison, Galileo was able to write extensively leaving records of his discoveries for posterity. In spite of all he went through, he enjoyed writing at the end, and because he was a visionary, he knew he was leaving the world a legacy. Many throughout history have criticized Galileo for not "dying" for the truth; but this is naïve and unfair, for those that criticize without knowing any better would have probably done the same.

This man's life caused me to lose sleep for three days as I felt the ordeals Galileo went through as if they were my own; and I got really close to his soul. I, a person born centuries apart, got to be his close friend through astrology. This experience that fascinated me, transformed me!

The Bible mentions the attributes of love:

"Love is patient, love is kind. It does not envy, it does not boast, it is not proud. It does not dishonor others, it is not self-seeking, it is not easily angered, it keeps no record of wrongs. Love does not delight in evil but rejoices with the truth. It always protects, always trusts, always hopes, always perseveres" *(Corinthians 13:4).*

Although we have heard, seen, and been told that every person is unique, we often assume everyone is like us; they should think and react like us. We tend to criticize and judge other people when their reactions to life's experiences are not the reactions we would have had. However, when we realize through astrology that people have different motivations, and attitudes as revealed by their birth chart, tolerance grows in us through the understanding of the different life circumstances people face according to the interplay of the energies affecting them. If we insist in thinking everyone else is just like us, we are missing the point which is that we, ourselves, must also go through personal growth by learning sympathy, compassion, and the appreciation of the different motivations, and goals revealed in our own horoscope, as well as the horoscopes of other people we now have the tools to examine and understand.

Knowing what makes us prone to like someone or not by looking at the astrology charts of the people involved, gives us the insight of the apparently irrational reactions we encounter when we deal with others. From total ignorance, when we do not know any better, we can go to an understanding of behaviors, and eventually acquire the spiritual attributes of patience, tolerance, kindness, and even love; because there is a point when we realize we are all essentially the same, in spite of the different energies that affect us; and that we are all here to learn. When we get it, either through deep meditation, or through numerology, or astrology, we gain the power to transcend, because knowledge is power; and, understanding coupled with love will lead us into the kingdom of Heaven that is within ourselves.

Conclusion

Astrology is a language of correspondence, a discovered natural science through which we can find the natural potentials indicated in a planetary natal horoscope of a person, city, country, or event, and make them flourish. We not only have the opportunity of gaining the understanding of others, and personal knowledge, but the attributes of the Inner self which are freely offered within this divine science, as we learn to relate to others, and develop tolerance, respect, and kindness. When we place ourselves in other people's shoes, and feel what they feel, love can transform us.

Astrology, at first seen as intellectual, becomes spiritual when it shows us how our natural influences can and should be used for the benefit of mankind. It becomes divine when we transcend the intellectual to follow the spiritual path as it takes us to the Ultimate Truth, because when we are open to receive, the knowledge we possess will lead us into finding our real identity, wisdom in conjunction to love, our

True self that is closer than hands and feet, God.

Works Cited

American Federation of Astrologers. *AFA Superstar Course in Astrology*. 2010. Print.

Astrodienst. *Persona Charts. Twelve (Archetypal) personalities*. Web.

Bailey, Alice. *Esoteric Astrology. A Treatise On The Seven Rays*. Lucis Trust. 1951. Web.

Doane, Doris Chase. *The Versatility of Astrology. It's Place In Your Life*. American Federation of Astrologers. 1997. Print.

----. *Astrology's Wide Influence*. American Federation of Astrologers. 2001. Print.

Golden, Carl. *The 12 Common Archetypes*. Soulcraft.co. Web.

Heindel, Max. *Simplified Scientific Astrology*. Murine Press. 2008. Kindle.

Holy Bible: *King James Version*. The National Bible Press. Philadelphia. 1944. Print.

Holy Bible*: New International Version*. Biblica Inc. 2011.

   Web.

Kotsos, Tania. *The Seven Universal Laws Explained*. Mind

   Your Reality. Web.

Louis, Anthony. *Horary Astrology Plain & Simple*.

Llewellyn Publications. Woodbury, MN. 2010. Print.

Hall, Manly P. *The Secret Teachings Of All Ages*. Originally

   self-Published in 1928. Kindle.

March, Marion D & Joan McEvers, *The Only Way to Learn*

   Astrology. Vol 1: Basic Principles. Second Edition.

   ACS Publications Starcrafts LLC. 2008. Print.

Masters, Paul Leon. *Master's degree curriculum. 2 vols*.

   Burbank, CA: Burbank printing, 2012. Print

Matt, Daniel C. *Kabbalah and Contemporary Cosmology:*

   Discovering the Resonance. Rosicrucian Digest.

Supreme Grand Lodge of AMORC, Rosicrucian Park, San

   Jose, CA. No. 2-2012. Vol 90-No.2. Kindle.

Metaphysical Zone. *Scorpio*. Wed.

Mulligan, Bob. *The Five Gifts of Astrology*. Unpublished
Article written for The Mountain Astrologer.
Astro.com. 2016.

Swedenborg, Emmanuel. *Heaven and Its Wonders and Hell
from things heard and seen*. Translated by John C.
Ager. Standard Edition. Swedenborg Foundation,
2009. Kindle.

Wikipedia. The Free Encyclopedia. *Life and work of
Reinhold Ebertin*. Web.

Who2 Biographies. *Galileo Galilei Biography*. Web.

www.ingramcontent.com/pod-product-compliance
Lightning Source LLC
Chambersburg PA
CBHW060226290526
45789CB00003B/1431